POCKET PICTURES

Northern England

Graeme Peacock

MYRIAD

LONDON

Berwick Trapped inside the Elizabethan walls of 1596 that enclose the town, much of Berwick-upon-Tweed's ancient street pattern still survives. The Royal Border Bridge, also known as the Railway Bridge, was designed by Robert Stephenson.

Lindisfarne Castle The posts in front of the castle are the remains of a jetty where lime was loaded onto ships bound for Dundee. In 1902 the castle was bought by Edward Hudson, founder of *Country Life*, and converted into a home.

Bamburgh Castle Perched on its huge rock, Bamburgh Castle can be seen for miles around; it dominates the village below, clustered around its wooded green. The churchyard has a monument to Grace Darling together with the graves of victims of shipwrecks. The first known fortification here was a wooden palisade built around 547.

The Farne Islands The Farne Islands are owned by the National Trust and consist of a group of islands 2.5 miles (4km) off the fishing village of Seahouses; between 15 and 28 islands are visible depending on the state of the tide. The islands form one of Britain's most important seabird sanctuaries. The closest island is Inner Farne and the furthest out, at 4.4 miles (7km) from the shore, is Knivestone. The chapel on Inner Farne is built on the site of St Cuthbert's Oratory. It was from the Longstone lighthouse situated on one of the outer Farne islands that Grace Darling and her father rowed out to rescue the survivors of the ship-wrecked *Forfarshire*. The lighthouse was built between 1825 and 1826.

Seahouses This working port grew out of the village of North Sunderland when local fishermen built their "sea houses" by the side of the harbour. The arched building in the photograph is a relic of the lime industry which flourished here until the 1850s; its flat top was a carriage ramp for a railway which carried materials to and from the port. Later in the century lime production declined and the fishing industry took over, fuelled by the demand for herring.

Dunstanburgh Today the most notable feature of Dunstanburgh Castle is the Lilburn Tower, which is visible for miles around. Built in 1323, the castle's ground floor held provisions while the upper floor provided accommodation for the garrison. The panoramic view from the castle ruins show the importance of Dunstanburgh as a defensive fortification.

Alnwick Known as the "Windsor of the North", the rolling fields and "natural" landscape of Alnwick is the work of the famous landscape gardener Lancelot "Capability" Brown who laid out the grounds in the 18th century. A local man, he was born at nearby Kirkharle. Alnwick Castle has one of the largest walled gardens in the world. One of its most impressive features is the Grand Cascade (right).

Alnwick The marketplace in Alnwick has long been a meeting place for the people of the town and dates back to the 1200s. With its cafes, shops, cobbled surface and market cross the area is the ideal location for the town's music festivals and craft and farmer's markets. Standing some 83ft (25m) high the fine fluted stone Tenantry Column – known locally as the "Farmers' Folly" – has an internal staircase leading to a gallery at the top. It was built in 1816 by local tenants to thank the duke for lowering their rents. The duke decided that if they could afford this gesture, they could afford the rents and he promptly raised them again!

Belsay Hall Sir Charles Monck was greatly influenced by the arts of the ancient Greeks. In 1817 he decided to build a Grecian-style house on his estate and employed some of the finest craftsmen to do so. Belsay Hall has one of the most beautiful gardens in Northumberland. It is full of corridors, arches and ravines with vines, ferns, palms and exotic and rare plants. In the late 19th and early 20th centuries Sir Charles' grandson Sir Arthur Middleton extended the garden and introduced rhododendrons and other plants new to the country.

Alnmouth Cross This cross on the southern side of the Aln estuary marks the site of the original village church of Alnmouth.

Warkworth Castle Built on a loop of the river Coquet, Warkworth was originally a wooden fortress constructed after the Norman Conquest. During the Middle Ages the wooden structure was gradually replaced by strong stone battlements. The resident Percy family took up arms against Elizabeth I. Thomas Percy, the 7th Earl was executed and Warkworth fell into disrepair.

Morpeth The river Wansbeck flows sedately through Morpeth, one of the most important market towns of Northumberland. The footbridge shown here is built on the abutments of the medieval bridge which was destroyed in 1832.

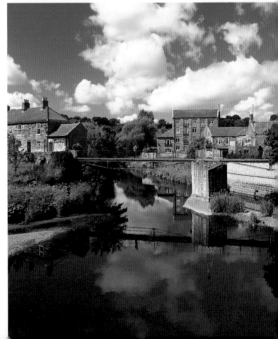

Chillingham This medieval castle sits close to the border with Scotland. The large cannons at the front and the remains of a moat bear witness to the fact that the building played a major part in the battles between England and Scotland. Now a stately home, Chillingham Castle is reputed to be one of the most haunted houses in the county. Amongst the ghosts is Lady Mary Berkeley whose rustling dress can still be heard along the corridors and stairs accompanied by a chilling blast of air.

Wallington Hall Work on this magnificent Palladian-style country house began in 1783; it is set amongst 100 acres of parkland with ornamental lakes, lawns and walled gardens, the work of the landscape gardener Capability Brown. The castle that previously occupied the site was owned by the famous Fenwick family of Northumberland.

Hadrian's Wall This massive structure was begun in AD122 and stretched 73.5 miles (117km) from Wallsend on the Tyne to the shores of the Solway Firth. A great deal of the middle section of the wall is largely intact and along its length are the ruins of a number of forts and milecastles. The Romans made use of the steep slopes of the countryside, including the Whin Sill escarpment, as a major defensive element in the construction and siting of the wall.

Housesteads Built at the height of the Roman Empire, Housesteads is the best-preserved example of a Roman fort in the country. It held a garrison of around 1,000 men, most of whom were German auxiliaries. Unlike other forts along the wall, Housesteads is built on quite a noticeable slope; the Romans sited their granaries at the highest part of the fort to keep the food inside dry. By the 13th century, Housesteads became a hiding place for reivers (cross-border raiders) and the cattle they had stolen.

Kielder Water The largest artificial lake in Europe, Kielder Water holds a staggering 200 billion litres of water and supplies the people and the industries of the north-east. Kielder Castle was built in 1775 as a shooting lodge for the Duke of Northumberland and now acts as the main visitor centre for the park, which has become a centre for recreational activities such as sailing, canoeing, cycling and birdwatching. The reservoir is surrounded by the vast Kielder Forest, the largest planted forest in Europe.

Hexham Abbey There has been a church on this site for over 1300 years. In 674 Wilfrid, Bishop of York, who was educated at Lindisfarne, established a Benedictine abbey here. In 875 the building was largely destroyed by the Vikings and it was not until about 1050 that a church was rebuilt on the site. This in turn was replaced in the early 13th century by an Augustinian priory and it is this church that we see today. The Saxon crypt and apse is all that remains of Wilfrid's original abbey. Since the Dissolution, the abbey has been used as the parish church of Hexham.

Breamish Valley This remote and wild valley is situated on the eastern edge of the Northumberland National Park with the tiny settlement of Ingram at its heart.

Cheviot Hills These rolling hills straddle the Scottish-English border and stretch across the northern half of Northumberland ending in the valley of the river Coquet. The hills are criss-crossed with bridleways, many marking the routes of ancient cattle-droving routes used in the past by herdsmen taking their animals to market.

Elsdon The Vicar's pele tower at Elsdon was built around 1400. The village also has the spectacular remains of a Norman motte and is noted for its large sloping green and the nearby Winter's Gibbet. The battle of Otterburn was fought nearby in 1388 and some of the dead were buried under the historic parish church of St Cuthbert.

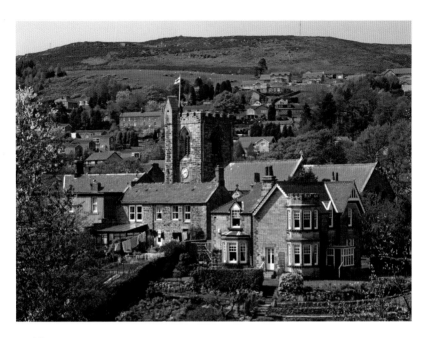

Rothbury With its sloping green shaded by sycamore trees, Rothbury is known as the capital of Coquetdale and serves a vast area of rural Northumberland. Its proximity to the beautiful Simonside Hills and the Lordenshaws hill fort make it a popular destination for visitors and locals alike. The Anglo-Saxons had a royal burgh here and the town was an ancient barony passing through various owners before coming into the hands of the Percy family in the 1330s.

Cragside With its mixture of German, French and Old English styles, Cragside has a majestic appearance and is surrounded by a 1000-acre forest garden. In fact with its hot and cold running water, fire alarms, telephones and a Turkish bath it was known as "The Palace of the Magician". Home to William Armstrong, the north-east's leading industrialist of his day, the house was begun in 1869 and finished in 1884. It was the first house in the world to be lit and powered by hydro-electricity. Lakes were created to make stunning vistas for which the estate is famous.

Seaton Sluice Lying at the southern border of the Northumberland coastline at the mouth of Seaton Burn, Seaton Sluice is made up of two separate villages, Seaton Sluice and Old Hartley. In the 17th century the mouth of Seaton Burn was treacherous and awkward for craft wanting to use the port. To alleviate the problem, in 1660 Sir Ralph Delaval built a stone pier to create a harbour. In 1690 Sir Ralph added sluice gates which closed as the incoming tide filled the harbour. At low tide the sluice gates were opened and a powerful flood of water flushed the harbour clean.

Blyth To the north and south of Blyth's harbour entrance are beautiful wide open beaches backed by sand dunes. Like many other ports in Northumberland, Blyth owes its present size to the development of the coal industry; exports of coal from the port started in the early 18th century and continued until the 1960s. The development of the port was accelerated in 1847 when a railway line was built linking it with collieries at Seghill. Nine large wind turbines erected in 1992 stretch out along the East Pier.

St Mary's Lighthouse

Lit up at night, St Mary's Lighthouse not only makes a beautiful reflection in the rock pools at low tide but also reveals the causeway which crosses the rocks surrounding the island. Built in 1898 and some 120ft (36.5m) high, the lighthouse has a birdwatching hide and visitor centre open to the public. As well as being a popular recreational destination it houses permanent and changing exhibitions and offers educational facilities. It is thought that the monks from Tynemouth had a chapel on the north side of the island and also a tower with an additional storey where a lantern was kept burning.

Cullercoats The colourful lifeboat station at Cullercoats is a well-loved feature of the beach. The lifeboat station here was established in 1852. Cullercoats is popular with Tynesiders and the town was particularly attractive to artists in the later years of the 19th century; work by the "Cullercoats Group" is now sought after by collectors and features in many collections in galleries and museums.

North Shields The fish quay at North Shields with its distinctive lighthouse is one of the best-known views in the north-east. Although much diminished from earlier days, fishing is still important here. To the south is the Souter Lighthouse and the Whitburn Coastal Park; to the north is the Leas – two and a half miles of cliffs, beaches and grassland with spectacular views.

Tynemouth Priory Perched on a clifftop, Tynemouth Priory is protected both by the sea and Tynemouth Castle, and is one of the largest fortified sites in the country. Originally the site was occupied by a 7th-century Saxon church, renowned as the burial place of St Oswin, king and martyr. The early monastery was sacked by the Danes in 800. The present buildings date from 1085 when a group of Benedictine monks from the abbey at St Albans arrived here; the monastery was finally completed at the end of the 13th century. The monks amassed great wealth from the coal industry which they used to finance the building work. Tynemouth Longsands stretches northwards backed by the town and sand dunes. The beach is very popular for those wanting to bathe, surf or simply relax. Nearby is a park, sealife centre, toy museum and shops, making it an ideal seaside destination. The cliffs at Tynemouth

are an excellent vantage point from which to watch ships entering the Tyne estuary, especially when magnificent sailing ships call at Newcastle in the annual Tall Ships Race.

Tyne bridges Crossing places on the Tyne between Newcastle and Gateshead hold a special place in the history of the north-east; these bridges have performed a vitally important role in the region's social and economic development. Each of the bridges has its own story to tell. The Swing Bridge opened in 1876 and was specially designed to allow large ships to pass upriver. The High Level Bridge, which opened in 1850, is one of the most important structures in the history of the British railway system. Robert Stephenson's bridge brought Newcastle into the London-Edinburgh railway link and confirmed the East Coast line as the major rail route between the two cities. Opened by George V in 1928 the Tyne Bridge is used by approximately 60,000 vehicles a day and was originally intended to have massive triumphal arches at each end. It is now associated with the swarming mass of runners crossing it as part of the Great North Run.

Millennium Bridge Opened in 2001, this spectacular footbridge links Newcastle Quay with the Sage and Baltic arts centres on the other side of the river. Nicknamed the "blinking eye", it can be raised in just four minutes to allow ships to pass underneath.

Earl Grey's monument The man from whom Grey Street gets its name, prime minister Earl Grey, is celebrated in a monument sited at the top of Grainger Street. The twice life-size statue was sculpted in 1838 by Edward Hodges Bailey, who was also responsible for Nelson's statue in Trafalgar Square. In the 19th century there were lights on top of the monument which were lit in the event of an accident occurring in the city: red lights indicated fatalities; white lights meant that all the participants had survived. The low platform at the base of the monument is a popular meeting place for shoppers.

Castle Keep The keep is all that remains today of the "new castle" that gave the city its name. It was constructed as part of the rebuilding in stone of the castle carried out by Henry II and took 10 years to complete. Even today, this structure gives an impression of immense military power. Newcastle Corporation supplied cannons to the keep to be fired on ceremonial occasions. This ended in tragedy in 1812 when one of the cannons exploded and a gunner was blown over the parapet.

Civic Centre Bathed in a blue light that seems to represent the waters of the Tyne, Newcastle's Civic Centre reflects much of the history and culture of this great city. Twelve seahorse heads cast in bronze, part of Newcastle's coat of arms, adorn the top of the tower. The heads are approximately 5ft (1.5m) in diameter. Sixteen feet (5m) up the exterior wall is a sandstone statue of the river god with water pouring out of his outstretched hand.

Northumberland University The striking Law, Business and Design School buildings at the University of Northumbria are clad in a stainless steel mesh frame to reduce over-heating on sunny days. The city has two universities – the universities of Newcastle and Northumbria; the campuses of both are located close to the city centre.

Hoppings The huge fairground called the Hoppings is best seen at night when tens of thousands of coloured lightbulbs burn brightly across the Town Moor. The Newcastle Hoppings is Europe's largest travelling fair and each year attracts hordes of visitors to the Moor in the last week of June. Local folklore has it that the rain that often accompanies the fair is the result of a Romany curse. The Temperance Fair held on the Town Moor was the forerunner of the Hoppings.

Angel of the North Constructed from sections transported to the site in 1998 and overlooking the A1, it is estimated that at least 90,000 motorists a day pass Antony Gormley's Angel of the North.

Souter lighthouse This distinctive red-and-white lighthouse is on the coast road in Whitburn. Built in 1871 it is now a fascinating museum depicting the life and workings of a Victorian lighthouse.

Marsden Rocks Renowned for the thousands of pairs of seabirds that nest here, these are some of the most dramatic rock formations in Britain. The shape of the rocks changed dramatically in 1996 when the arch that joined the present two stacks collapsed into the sea. The Marsden Rocks are reput-edly haunted by the ghost of John the Jibber. He died a lingering death suspended in a bucket halfway down the cliff, having betrayed his fellow smugglers to the customs men.

Arbeia Roman Fort Four miles east of Hadrian's Wall this fort guarded the entrance to the river Tyne. Constructed around AD160 as a military supply depot for all of the 17 forts along the wall, the west gate of the fort has been reconstructed to house a museum.

Sunderland The Winter Gardens house a superb botanical collection of over 1,500 plants of 146 species in naturalistic settings under a single-span 98.5ft (30m) dome. The gardens display samples of many important plants from around the world and visitors can take a staircase or scenic lift up to a tree-top walkway where they can look down into an amazing rainforest canopy below. The Winter Gardens are linked to Sunderland's remodelled museum and the upgraded and re-landscaped Mowbray Park in the city. Visitors enter the museum via a striking new glazed entrance which leads into the "museum street".

Set on the north bank of the river Wear, the award-winning National Glass Centre is a stunning building and acts as a base for artists to meet and create new products and artworks.

Tree sculpture Just upstream from the Wearside Bridge is *Shadows in Another Light* (right) a sculpture in which the shadow cast by a tree represents a hammerhead crane – a piece of machinery unique to the Sunderland dock area.

Penshaw Monument
Built in 1844 by private sub-scription and designed by John and Benjamin Green of New-castle, the Penshaw Monument is unusual in that it has no in-scription. Built in the form of a 100ft (30.5m) long, 50ft (15m) wide and 70ft (21m) high ruined Greek temple, the monu-ment is based on the Temple of Theseus in Athens.

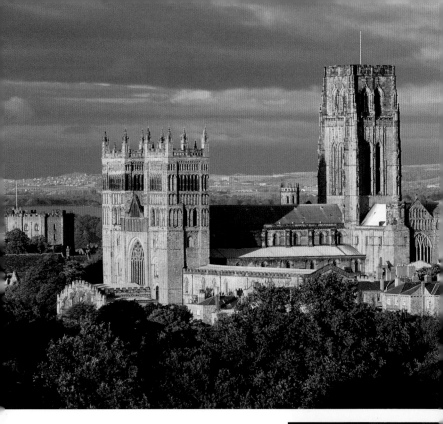

Durham Cathedral Begun by Bishop William of Calais in 1093, Durham Cathedral is an outstanding example of Romanesque architecture. Inside the cathedral, the nave is particularly striking for its massive spiral and zig-zag decorated columns and the larger multiple-columned compound piers which support the impressive diamond-ribbed vaulting of the ceiling high above. The cathedral has been a centre for pilgrimage throughout its 900-year history. It contains the tombs of St Cuthbert, the saintly seventh-century bishop of Lindisfarne and that of the Venerable Bede, the first English historian, which were placed there in 1370. There have been occasions over the centuries when the cathedral has suffered damage and vandalism. The 14th-century altar screen originally

contained 107 alabaster figures but many were vandalised in the 16th century. In 1650 further damage was caused when Cromwell imprisoned 4,000 Scots there. One of the most beautiful features of the cathedral today is the huge rose window with its central core depicting Christ surrounded by the apostles. The cloisters adjoin the south side of the cathedral and are clustered around a small square green known as the Cloister Garth.

Durham Castle This is a fine example of the Norman motte and bailey style of fortification. Building began in 1072 with a circular keep on top of the hill overlooking the town as a part of William the Conqueror's plan to pacify the region; the castle was enlarged in 1174. During the middle ages, Durham was one of a number of castles spread throughout the north to counter the threat of invasion from the Scots. Later it was taken over as the principal residence of the Bishops of Durham or the Prince Bishops as they were known, since they administered the county on behalf of the Crown. It was they who built the magnificent halls and chapel, rare survivors of secular Norman splendour. The medieval bishops continued to develop the castle and in the 17th century more lavish accommodation was provided.

Beamish The world-famous open air museum at Beamish was set up in 1970 and tells the story of the people of the north-east of England at two important points of their history – in 1825 and 1913. The museum is made up of old buildings from the region. Some, such as the Drift Mine, Home Farm and Pockerley Manor were already on the site; others have been brought from their original location and carefully reconstructed. There are no labels or glass cases at Beamish; the idea is to give visitors a realistic view of life in the past. Staff are dressed in costume and the feeling is much more of being part of a theatrical production than walking the aisles of a traditional museum.

Brancepeth Castle Built in the 11th century, Brancepeth Castle has played a major role in the history of the region. Originally the home of a Saxon lord, it eventually became the property of the Nevilles until confiscated by Elizabeth I. Sir Henry Bellaysyse, who owned the castle in the early 18th century, had a daughter, Mary, who became attracted to a local man, Bobby Shaftoe. Her love for Bobby became the subject of the famous north-eastern song.

Raby Castle One of the largest and most impressive of England's medieval castles, Raby is famous for its beautiful walled gardens and deer park. King Canute owned the estate in the early 11th century and may well have built the first castle here. The present building was begun by John, 3rd Baron Nevill, in about 1360. The castle includes a sturdy gatehouse, complete with portcullis and "murder holes" for pouring oil on attackers.

Bishop's Palace Auckland Castle has been the home of the Bishops of Durham – the "Bishop's Palace" – for over 800 years. Originally, this was a banqueting hall and hunting lodge built in the 12th century and was gradually developed for the Prince Bishops into one of the most ornate palaces in Britain. The magnificent chapel is believed to be the largest private place of worship in Europe.

Barnard Castle Perched high on a steep bank overlooking the river Tees, Barnard Castle was first built around the year 1095 and later fortified again by Bernard Balliol in 1135. The castle gave its name to the town that grew up alongside it.

Bowes Museum This famous museum in Barnard Castle originated in a private foundation created between 1862 and 1875 by John and Josephine Bowes. It was conceived and purpose-built as a public art gallery by the French architect Jules Pellechet and opened in 1892. The building is designed in the style of a French chateau and has public galleries on three floors and a collection of European fine and decorative arts from the middle ages to early Victorian times. There is particular emphasis on the arts of France including items from the Bowes' home in Paris. Perhaps the best known exhibit in the museum is the famous Silver Swan, a life-size musical automaton comprising a clockwork mechanism covered in silver plumage above a music box. Bowes has some of the best collections of European art, particularly Italian and Spanish art, in Britain.

Lumley Castle This magnificent building is set within nine acres of parkland overlooking the river Wear near Chester-le-Street. It was built in 1392 as a manor house and was later converted by Sir Ralph Lumley into the castle that can be seen today. Sir Ralph built four great corner towers and the intervening buildings as well as the main gateway on the east.

Egglestone Abbey The ruins of Egglestone Abbey perch above a steep slope overlooking the river Tees just south of Barnard Castle. The abbey lies in the grounds of Egglestone Hall and was founded in 1195. In the 19th century much of the abbey was pulled down and its stone used for building.

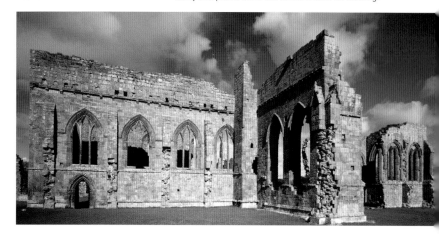

Tees Valley The river Tees rises in the foothills of the north Pennines and flows east to meet the sea at Teesmouth, south of Hartlepool. The upper valley is characterised by heather-clad moorland and rolling farmland interspersed with the scattered ruins of the area's industrial past – in particular leadmining. This upland area is rich in nationally renowned beauty spots which include the dramatic waterfalls at High Force and Cauldron Snout. It then flows past historic towns and villages which include Middleton-in-Teesdale and Darlington; in its final stretch it passes through towns and cities such as Stockton-on-Tees, Middlesbrough and Hartlepool which form the industrial heartland of the region.

Stockton-on-Tees The Infinity Footbridge is reflected in the waters of the river Tees. The Tees Barrage has created a stretch of clean, high-quality deep water making the river more suitable for recreational uses.

43

Middlesbrough The famous Transporter Bridge dominates the city's skyline and, with a clearance of 160ft (48m), was originally designed to allow tall ships to pass beneath. Opened on October 17 1911 by Prince Arthur of Connaught, this unique bridge with its central cradle that ferries cars and pedestrians across the river has become Middlesbrough's icon. Its gondola can carry 200 people or six cars and one minibus across the river in just two and a half minutes. A short distance upstream is the Newport Bridge – the first vertical lift bridge in Britain – built so that the central section can be raised to allow ships to pass beneath.

It was opened in 1934. Middlesbrough grew rapidly after the discovery of iron ore in the Cleveland Hills prompted local businessmen to build a blast furnace in the town. Soon the town was famous as the steel manufacturing centre of the region. The "bottle of notes" sculpture stands next to the Middlesbrough Institute of Art.

Hartlepool Until the second quarter of the 19th century Hartlepool was a collection of small villages, sand dunes and marshes. By the end of the century it had become the fifth largest shipping port in the UK. Today Hartlepool Marina, with the Historic Quay, is one of the major signs of the regeneration of the town. Dominating the quay are the triple masts of HMS *Trincomalee*. Built of teak in India in 1817 she is the oldest fighting ship still afloat in the country.

Saltburn Completed in 1869, Saltburn Pier is the only remaining pier on the north-east coast. The pier can be reached from the town by the cliff lift which was opened in 1884. The lift is the oldest water-balanced lift in the country and the cabins have been refurbished with stained-glass windows.

Durham skyline The world-famous castle and cathedral are jammed together on a narrow site created by the river Wear as it flows in a hairpin bend. This collection of historic buildings has been designated as a World Heritage Site.